APPLE AIRPODS PRO 2 WIRELESS EARBUDS USER GUIDE

Comprehensive Tips for Optimal Performance

MARCUS T. HOOKS

COPYRIGHT

TABLE OF CONTENTS

INTRODUCTION
The Apple AirPods Pro 2 Wireless Earbuds User Guide

Wireless earbuds have revolutionized the way we listen to music, connect to calls, and interact with our devices. Among the leading names in the audio technology landscape, Apple stands tall with its innovative and user-friendly products. The AirPods Pro 2, Apple's latest iteration in the AirPods lineup, represents the pinnacle of wireless earbud technology, combining cutting-edge features with an unmatched ease of use. This guide is designed to take you through every aspect of these remarkable earbuds, ensuring you can harness their full potential and elevate your audio experience.

The Evolution of AirPods

When Apple first introduced the AirPods in 2016, it marked the beginning of a new era in wireless audio. The seamless integration with Apple's ecosystem and the simplicity of their design quickly captured the imagination of users worldwide. Over the years, Apple has refined and improved upon this initial offering, with each iteration bringing new features and innovations. The AirPods Pro 2 builds on this legacy, offering significant enhancements in sound quality, comfort, and functionality. From spatial audio to advanced noise cancellation, the AirPods Pro 2 are designed to cater to the needs of the most discerning audiophiles and tech enthusiasts.

Why Choose the AirPods Pro 2?

With countless wireless earbuds on the market, you might wonder what sets the AirPods Pro 2 apart. The answer lies in their holistic design philosophy, which combines superior hardware, intelligent software, and seamless ecosystem integration. These earbuds are not just about listening to music—they are about experiencing it in a way that feels personal, immersive, and effortless.

Here are some of the standout features that make the AirPods Pro 2 a compelling choice:

- **Active Noise Cancellation and Transparency Mode:** Block out distractions or stay aware of your surroundings with a single touch.

- **Adaptive Transparency:** A new feature that minimizes the intensity of loud noises while maintaining situational awareness.

- **Spatial Audio:** Enjoy an immersive, theater-like experience with head tracking technology that adjusts sound based on your movements.

- **H2 Chip:** The next-generation Apple chip delivers better performance, longer battery life, and improved sound quality.

- **Enhanced Fit:** With four sizes of silicone tips, the AirPods Pro 2 ensure a perfect fit for all ear shapes and sizes.

Purpose of This Guide

While the AirPods Pro 2 are intuitive to use, their advanced features and customization options can be overwhelming for new users. This guide aims to simplify every aspect of your AirPods Pro 2 experience. Whether you're a first-time user or upgrading from a previous version, this book will serve as your trusted companion, walking you through the setup process, explaining how to use the various features, and troubleshooting any issues you may encounter.

Here's what you can expect to learn:

- How to unbox and set up your AirPods Pro 2 for the first time.

- Tips for optimizing the sound quality to suit your preferences.

- How to pair your AirPods with Apple and non-Apple devices.

- Detailed instructions for using Active Noise Cancellation, Transparency Mode, and other features.

- Guidance on caring for and maintaining your AirPods to extend their lifespan.

Who This Guide Is For

This guide is for anyone who owns or is considering purchasing the AirPods Pro 2. It's designed to cater to a wide audience, including:

- **Beginners:** If you're new to wireless earbuds or the Apple ecosystem, this guide will help you get started with confidence.

- **Advanced Users:** For those upgrading from an earlier version of AirPods or other earbuds, we'll explore advanced features and customization options.

- **Troubleshooters:** If you've run into issues with your AirPods, this guide will provide solutions to common problems and advice on when to seek professional support.

The AirPods Pro 2—A Symphony of Technology

At the heart of the AirPods Pro 2 lies Apple's new H2 chip, a technological marvel that powers most of the earbuds' impressive features. This chip not only enhances sound quality but also improves Active Noise Cancellation, enabling a quieter, more focused listening experience. Additionally, the H2 chip allows for more efficient energy management, resulting in longer battery life. With up to six hours of listening time on a single charge and an additional 30 hours provided by the charging case, you can enjoy your AirPods Pro 2 throughout your day without worrying about running out of power.

Another standout feature is the advanced Spatial Audio with personalized settings. By scanning the shape of your ear using your iPhone, the AirPods Pro 2 can create a custom sound profile tailored to your unique auditory preferences. This means that no matter what you're listening to—music, movies, podcasts, or phone calls—the experience feels more vivid and lifelike.

Seamless Integration with the Apple Ecosystem

One of the reasons Apple products are so popular is their seamless integration across the ecosystem, and the AirPods Pro 2 are no exception. Pairing them with your iPhone, iPad, Mac, or Apple Watch is a breeze, thanks to the automatic pairing feature. Once connected, you can effortlessly switch between devices without manually adjusting the settings. This level of convenience is unmatched and makes the AirPods Pro 2 an essential accessory for anyone already invested in Apple's ecosystem.

A Commitment to Sustainability

Apple has made significant strides in ensuring that its products are environmentally friendly, and the AirPods Pro 2 are a testament to this commitment. The charging case now includes a lanyard loop for added convenience, and the materials used in its construction are more sustainable than ever. Additionally, Apple offers a robust recycling program, allowing users to responsibly dispose of their old devices when upgrading to the latest model.

What's New in the AirPods Pro 2?

If you're familiar with the original AirPods Pro, you might be wondering what's new in the second generation. Here are some of the most exciting upgrades:

- **Improved Sound Quality:** The H2 chip and custom-built drivers deliver richer bass and clearer high frequencies.

- **Adaptive EQ:** Automatically adjusts the audio to fit the shape of your ear for a more natural listening experience.

- **Enhanced Noise Cancellation:** Blocks twice as much noise compared to the previous model.

- **Precision Finding:** With the Find My app, you can locate your AirPods Pro 2 and charging case more easily than ever before.

- **Touch Controls for Volume:** Swipe up or down on the stem to adjust the volume without reaching for your device.

Join the Wireless Revolution

The AirPods Pro 2 are more than just a pair of earbuds—they're a statement of how far technology has come in enhancing our everyday lives. Whether you're commuting, working out, or simply relaxing at home, these earbuds provide an unparalleled audio experience. This guide will equip you with all the knowledge you need to master your AirPods Pro 2, so you can enjoy the perfect blend of innovation, comfort, and convenience that they offer.

CHAPTER 1

Apple AirPods Pro 2 Wireless Earbuds

Wireless earbuds have transformed the way we experience audio, offering a blend of convenience, technology, and style. Among the leaders in this space is Apple, a brand synonymous with innovation and user-centric design. With the launch of the Apple AirPods Pro 2, Apple continues its legacy of redefining the listening experience. This guide delves deep into the AirPods Pro 2, exploring their features, improvements, and the reasons why they stand out in an ever-evolving market of wireless audio solutions. Whether you're a first-time user or an experienced audiophile, this guide will help you maximize your AirPods Pro 2 experience.

Overview of Features and Improvements

The Apple AirPods Pro 2 represent a significant leap forward in wireless earbud technology. With enhancements across hardware, software, and functionality, these earbuds cater to a wide range of users. Below is an in-depth look at the standout features and improvements:

- **Active Noise Cancellation (ANC):** The AirPods Pro 2 boast advanced ANC technology that blocks out twice as much noise compared to the first generation. Whether you're on a noisy commute or working in a bustling coffee shop, the improved noise cancellation ensures an immersive and distraction-free listening experience.

- **Transparency Mode with Adaptive Transparency:** Transparency Mode has been upgraded to Adaptive Transparency, which intelligently reduces the intensity of loud sounds like sirens or construction noise while maintaining situational awareness.

- **H2 Chip:** At the heart of the AirPods Pro 2 is Apple's H2 chip, a next-generation processor that enhances sound quality, improves battery life, and powers advanced features like Spatial Audio and Adaptive EQ.

- **Spatial Audio:** Experience a theater-like soundstage with personalized Spatial Audio. Using your iPhone's TrueDepth camera, the AirPods Pro 2 create a custom sound profile tailored to the unique shape of your ears.

- **Touch Controls:** A new addition to the AirPods Pro 2 is touch-sensitive volume control. Simply swipe up or down on the stem to adjust the volume without needing to reach for your device.

- **Improved Fit and Comfort:** The AirPods Pro 2 come with four sizes of silicone ear tips, ensuring a secure and comfortable fit for all ear shapes. The lightweight design makes them ideal for extended wear.

- **Enhanced Sound Quality:** Custom-built drivers and amplifiers deliver richer bass, clearer highs, and a more balanced sound profile. The Adaptive EQ adjusts audio in real-time based on the fit and seal of the ear tips.

- **Longer Battery Life:** Enjoy up to six hours of listening time on a single charge, with an additional 30 hours provided by the MagSafe charging case. The case now features a built-in speaker for easier location using the Find My app.

- **Sustainability:** Apple has incorporated more recycled materials into the AirPods Pro 2 and offers a robust recycling program for older devices, reflecting its commitment to environmental responsibility.

These features make the AirPods Pro 2 not just an accessory but a comprehensive audio solution designed for modern lifestyles.

Who This Guide Is For

This user guide is designed to cater to a broad audience, ensuring that every user—regardless of their familiarity with Apple products or wireless earbuds—can fully utilize the capabilities of the AirPods Pro 2. Below are the primary groups who will benefit from this guide:

1. **First-Time Users:** If you're new to wireless earbuds, particularly the AirPods lineup, this guide will walk you through every step of the setup process. From unboxing to pairing with your devices, you'll find detailed instructions to help you get started.

2. **Experienced Apple Users:** For those upgrading from earlier AirPods models or other Apple devices, this guide highlights the new features and improvements of the AirPods Pro 2. Learn how to integrate these earbuds seamlessly into your existing Apple ecosystem.

3. **Audiophiles and Sound Enthusiasts:** With their superior sound quality and customizable audio settings, the AirPods Pro 2 are perfect for those who value high-fidelity audio. This guide covers tips and tricks for optimizing sound performance, from using Spatial Audio to tweaking the Adaptive EQ.

4. **Professionals and On-the-Go Users:** Whether you're taking calls, participating in virtual meetings, or listening to podcasts during your commute, the AirPods Pro 2 offer features tailored to productivity and convenience. This guide includes sections on managing calls, using Siri for hands-free commands, and troubleshooting common issues.

5. **Fitness Enthusiasts:** The AirPods Pro 2's sweat- and water-resistant design makes them ideal for workouts and outdoor activities. This guide explains how to secure the best fit and care for your earbuds to ensure durability.

6. **Troubleshooters and Tech Support Seekers:** If you encounter issues with your AirPods Pro 2, this guide provides troubleshooting tips and solutions for common problems, along with guidance on when to contact Apple Support.

By the end of this guide, you'll have a comprehensive understanding of your AirPods Pro 2, from their basic operations to advanced features. This user guide ensures that every aspect of your experience is covered, empowering you to make the most of these cutting-edge earbuds.

CHAPTER 2

Unboxing and Getting Started with the Apple AirPods Pro 2

The excitement of unboxing a new gadget is a feeling like no other, especially when it's something as innovative and high-performing as the Apple AirPods Pro 2. This chapter is designed to guide you through the initial stages of your AirPods Pro 2 experience, ensuring a smooth start to your journey with these exceptional wireless earbuds. From understanding what comes in the box to setting them up for the first time, you'll find all the information you need right here.

What's Included in the Box

The Apple AirPods Pro 2 come in a sleek and compact package that reflects Apple's commitment to minimalist design and sustainability. Opening the box, you will find the following components carefully arranged to provide a satisfying unboxing experience:

1. **AirPods Pro 2 Earbuds:**

   o The main stars of the show, the AirPods Pro 2 earbuds come pre-paired to the charging case and ready for use.

2. **MagSafe Charging Case:**

   o The redesigned charging case now features a built-in speaker and lanyard loop for added convenience. It also supports MagSafe and Qi wireless charging, as well as charging via a Lightning cable.

3. **Silicone Ear Tips (Four Sizes):**

   o To ensure a perfect fit for all users, the AirPods Pro 2 come with four sizes of silicone ear tips: XS, S, M, and L. Apple's Ear Tip Fit Test can help you select the ideal size for optimal comfort and sound quality.

4. **Lightning to USB-C Cable:**

   o A durable and efficient cable for wired charging of the MagSafe case. While the AirPods Pro 2 support wireless charging, this cable provides an alternative for faster and more reliable power delivery.

5. **Documentation:**

   o Inside the box, you'll find a Quick Start guide, warranty information, and safety instructions to help you get acquainted with your new device.

Inspecting the Contents

Before you proceed, take a moment to ensure that all items are present and in good condition. If anything is missing or damaged, contact Apple Support or the retailer from which you purchased your AirPods Pro 2.

Charging the Case and Earbuds

Before using your AirPods Pro 2 for the first time, it's essential to ensure they are fully charged. Proper charging not only optimizes performance but also helps you familiarize yourself with the charging process. Here's how to do it:

1. **Charging the Case:**

   o The MagSafe charging case can be charged in multiple ways:

- **Wireless Charging:** Place the case on a MagSafe or Qi-compatible wireless charging pad. The built-in LED indicator on the front of the case will light up to show the charging status.

- **Wired Charging:** Use the included Lightning to USB-C cable to connect the case to a power source. Plug the USB-C end into a compatible adapter or USB port.

o A full charge provides up to 30 additional hours of listening time for your AirPods Pro 2.

2. **Charging the Earbuds:**

o Place the earbuds inside the charging case. The case is designed to automatically charge the earbuds whenever they are docked. You'll know the earbuds are charging when the LED indicator on the case lights up.

o   A quick five-minute charge can provide up to one hour of listening time, making it convenient for users on the go.

Battery Indicator and Status

- The LED light on the front of the MagSafe charging case indicates the charging status:

    o   **Green:** Fully charged.

    o   **Amber:** Charging in progress.

    o   **Flashing White:** Ready to pair or reset.

To check the battery levels of both the case and earbuds, you can use your iPhone or iPad. Simply open the case near your device, and the battery status will appear on the screen.

Setting Up for the First Time

Setting up your AirPods Pro 2 is a seamless process, thanks to Apple's intuitive design and ecosystem integration. Whether you're pairing them with an iPhone, iPad, Mac, or even a non-Apple device, the steps are straightforward. Below, we outline the setup process for different scenarios:

1. **Pairing with an iPhone or iPad:**

   o Ensure your iPhone or iPad is updated to the latest version of iOS or iPadOS.

   o Open the MagSafe charging case with the AirPods inside and hold it near your device.

   o A setup animation will appear on your device's screen. Tap "Connect."

   o Follow the on-screen instructions to complete the setup. You can customize settings such as Spatial Audio during this process.

   o Once paired, the AirPods Pro 2 will automatically connect to all devices linked to your iCloud account.

2. **Pairing with a Mac:**

   o Open the Bluetooth preferences on your Mac.

   o Open the MagSafe charging case and press the setup button on the back until the LED flashes white.

   o Select "AirPods Pro 2" from the list of available devices and click "Connect."

3. **Pairing with Non-Apple Devices:**

   o The AirPods Pro 2 can also be paired with Android devices and other Bluetooth-enabled gadgets.

   o Open the MagSafe charging case and press the setup button on the back until the LED flashes white.

   o Enable Bluetooth on your device and select "AirPods Pro 2" from the available devices.

   o While some advanced features like Spatial Audio may not be available, the AirPods Pro 2 will function as high-quality wireless earbuds.

Customizing Your AirPods Pro 2

Once your AirPods Pro 2 are set up, you can personalize them to suit your preferences:

1. **Name Your AirPods:**

   o Open the Settings app on your iPhone or iPad.

   o Go to Bluetooth, tap the "i" icon next to your AirPods, and select "Name."

o Enter a custom name to easily identify your AirPods in the Bluetooth menu.

2. **Adjust Noise Control Settings:**

   o Use the Force Sensor on the AirPods stem to toggle between Active Noise Cancellation and Transparency Mode.

   o You can also customize the press-and-hold action for each earbud in the Settings app.

3. **Enable Spatial Audio:**

   o Open the Control Center on your iPhone or iPad.

   o Press and hold the volume slider, then tap "Spatial Audio" to enable it.

   o For a personalized experience, use your device's TrueDepth camera to create a custom Spatial Audio profile.

Testing Your AirPods

After setting up your AirPods Pro 2, it's a good idea to test their functionality:

- Play a song or podcast to check the sound quality.

- Test the Active Noise Cancellation and Transparency Mode in different environments.

- Make a phone call to ensure the microphones are working properly.

- Use Siri to verify hands-free voice command functionality.

Unboxing and setting up the Apple AirPods Pro 2 is an exciting and straightforward process that sets the stage for an exceptional audio experience. With their advanced features, customizable settings, and seamless integration with the Apple ecosystem, the AirPods Pro 2 are designed to elevate your daily routine. This chapter has provided a comprehensive guide to getting started, ensuring that you can enjoy your new earbuds to the fullest right out of the box. In the chapters that follow, we'll dive deeper into their features, controls, and tips for optimizing your usage.

CHAPTER 3

Connecting to Devices with the Apple AirPods Pro 2

One of the defining features of the Apple AirPods Pro 2 is their seamless connectivity, which ensures you can enjoy your audio experience across a variety of devices. Whether you're pairing them with an iPhone, iPad, or even non-Apple devices, the process is designed to be straightforward and efficient. This chapter provides an extensive guide on connecting your AirPods Pro 2 to different devices, including troubleshooting common issues that may arise during the process.

Pairing with iPhone and Other Apple Devices

The AirPods Pro 2 are designed to integrate effortlessly with Apple's ecosystem, making pairing with an iPhone or other Apple devices a breeze. Here's how to get started:

Step-by-Step Guide to Pairing with an iPhone:

1. **Ensure Compatibility and Update iOS:**

    o   Before pairing, ensure your iPhone is running the latest version of iOS. To check, go to

Settings > General > Software Update. If an
update is available, install it.

2. **Open the Charging Case:**

   o With your AirPods Pro 2 inside, open the
      MagSafe charging case and hold it near your
      iPhone. Ensure Bluetooth is enabled on your
      device (Settings > Bluetooth).

3. **Automatic Pairing Prompt:**

   o A setup animation will appear on your iPhone
      screen. Tap "Connect" to begin the pairing
      process. Follow any additional on-screen
      instructions, such as setting up Spatial Audio.

4. **Finalize Pairing:**

   o Once connected, your AirPods Pro 2 will be
      linked to your Apple ID. This means they'll
      automatically pair with other Apple devices
      signed in to the same iCloud account, such as
      your iPad, Mac, or Apple Watch.

Pairing with an iPad or Mac:

- **For iPad:** Follow the same steps as above. Open the case near your iPad, and a pairing prompt will appear. Tap "Connect" to complete the process.

- **For Mac:**

  1. Open System Settings on your Mac and navigate to Bluetooth.

  2. Open the AirPods Pro 2 charging case and press the setup button on the back until the LED flashes white.

  3. Select "AirPods Pro 2" from the list of available devices and click "Connect."

Switching Between Apple Devices:

Thanks to iCloud synchronization, switching between Apple devices is automatic. For instance, if you're listening to music on your iPhone and start watching a video on your iPad, the AirPods Pro 2 will transition seamlessly. If the switch doesn't happen automatically, you can manually select the AirPods in the Bluetooth menu or from the Control Center.

Connecting to Non-Apple Devices

While the AirPods Pro 2 are optimized for Apple's ecosystem, they can also be paired with non-Apple devices, such as Android smartphones, Windows PCs, and other Bluetooth-enabled gadgets. However, some advanced features like Spatial Audio and automatic switching may not be available.

Pairing with Android Devices:

1. **Enable Bluetooth:**

   o On your Android device, go to Settings > Connections > Bluetooth and ensure it is turned on.

2. **Activate Pairing Mode:**

   o Open the AirPods Pro 2 charging case and press the setup button on the back until the LED indicator flashes white.

3. **Select AirPods Pro 2:**

   o In the Bluetooth settings on your Android device, look for "AirPods Pro 2" under the list of available devices. Tap to connect.

4. **Confirm Connection:**

   o Once paired, your AirPods Pro 2 will function as regular Bluetooth earbuds. You can use them for calls, music, and more, albeit without some of the advanced Apple-exclusive features.

Pairing with Windows PCs:

1. **Open Bluetooth Settings:**

   o On your Windows PC, go to Settings > Devices > Bluetooth & Other Devices.

   o Turn on Bluetooth if it's not already enabled.

2. **Pair Your AirPods Pro 2:**

   o Open the AirPods case and press the setup button until the LED flashes white.

   o Click "Add Bluetooth or Other Device" on your PC and select "Bluetooth."

   o Choose "AirPods Pro 2" from the list of available devices.

3. **Confirm Connection:**

  o Once paired, you can use the AirPods Pro 2 for audio playback and calls. Adjust audio settings as needed in your PC's sound preferences.

Pairing with Smart TVs and Gaming Consoles:

While not all smart TVs and gaming consoles support Bluetooth audio, many modern devices do. Check your TV or console's Bluetooth settings to pair your AirPods Pro 2. Follow the same pairing process by putting the AirPods in pairing mode and selecting them from the list of available devices.

Troubleshooting Connection Issues

Despite Apple's emphasis on seamless connectivity, occasional issues can arise. Here's a guide to troubleshooting common connection problems:

1. AirPods Not Connecting to a Device:

• **Ensure Bluetooth is Enabled:** Verify that Bluetooth is turned on for the device you're trying to connect to.

- **Reset Your AirPods Pro 2:** Place the AirPods in the charging case and close the lid for 15 seconds. Open the lid and press the setup button on the back until the LED flashes white. Attempt to pair again.

- **Restart Your Device:** Sometimes, restarting your iPhone, Android device, or computer can resolve connectivity issues.

2. Frequent Disconnects:

- **Check Battery Levels:** Low battery can cause the AirPods to disconnect. Ensure both the earbuds and charging case are sufficiently charged.

- **Update Firmware:** Ensure your AirPods Pro 2 are running the latest firmware. Updates are automatically installed when connected to an Apple device with an active internet connection.

- **Reduce Interference:** Bluetooth performance can be affected by interference from other devices. Move closer to your connected device and minimize interference.

3. One Earbud Not Working:

- **Check Fit and Seal:** Ensure the earbud is properly seated in your ear.

- **Clean the Earbuds:** Dirt or debris on the speaker mesh can impact audio. Use a soft, lint-free cloth to clean the earbuds.

- **Reset the AirPods Pro 2:** Follow the reset procedure mentioned above.

4. Audio Quality Issues:

- **Adjust Device Settings:** Check the audio settings on your device to ensure proper playback configuration.

- **Re-pair the AirPods:** Remove the AirPods from your device's Bluetooth settings and pair them again.

5. AirPods Not Appearing in Bluetooth List:

- Ensure the AirPods are in pairing mode (LED flashing white).

- Restart the device and try again.

Tips for Optimizing Connectivity

- **Keep Devices Updated:** Ensure all devices, including your AirPods Pro 2, are running the latest software or firmware.

- **Enable Automatic Switching:** If you're using multiple Apple devices, make sure automatic switching is enabled in the Bluetooth settings.

- **Use "Find My" for Tracking:** If your AirPods Pro 2 go missing, use the Find My app to locate them easily.

The Apple AirPods Pro 2 offer unparalleled connectivity, designed to integrate seamlessly with Apple's ecosystem while remaining versatile enough to work with non-Apple devices. By following the steps outlined in this chapter, you can ensure a hassle-free pairing process and resolve any potential connectivity issues with ease. With these earbuds, staying connected has never been more effortless or enjoyable.

CHAPTER 4

Controls and Gestures on the Apple AirPods Pro 2

One of the most remarkable features of the Apple AirPods Pro 2 is their intuitive control system, which allows users to interact with their audio seamlessly. By integrating advanced sensors and touch controls, Apple ensures that users can manage playback, adjust volume, and customize gestures with ease. This chapter provides a comprehensive guide to mastering the controls and gestures of your AirPods Pro 2, ensuring you make the most of their advanced features.

Using the Force Sensor

The Force Sensor is a key component of the AirPods Pro 2's control system. Built into the stems of the earbuds, the Force Sensor allows users to perform various actions with simple presses. Here's how to use it effectively:

Basic Functions of the Force Sensor:

1. **Play and Pause Audio:**

    o   Press the Force Sensor once to play or pause your music, podcast, or video.

2. **Skip to the Next Track:**

   o Double-press the Force Sensor to skip to the next track.

3. **Go Back to the Previous Track:**

   o Triple-press the Force Sensor to return to the previous track or restart the current one.

4. **Answer or End Calls:**

   o Press the Force Sensor once to answer an incoming call or end an ongoing call.

5. **Switch Between Noise Control Modes:**

   o Press and hold the Force Sensor to toggle between Active Noise Cancellation and Transparency Mode.

Tips for Optimal Use:

- Ensure a secure fit in your ear to prevent accidental presses.

- Familiarize yourself with the tactile feedback of the Force Sensor to develop muscle memory for common actions.

The Force Sensor's simplicity and versatility make it an essential tool for controlling your AirPods Pro 2 without needing to access your device.

Touch Controls for Volume and Playback

The addition of touch-sensitive controls on the AirPods Pro 2 is a game-changer, offering users an easy way to adjust the volume directly from the earbuds. Here's how to use these touch controls effectively:

Adjusting Volume:

1. **Increase Volume:**

   o   Swipe upward on the stem of either earbud to raise the volume.

2. **Decrease Volume:**

   o   Swipe downward on the stem of either earbud to lower the volume.

3. **Volume Feedback:**

   o   Changes in volume are accompanied by audible tones to confirm adjustments.

Playback Controls:

In addition to the Force Sensor, touch controls provide another layer of convenience for managing playback:

- Combine touch gestures with Force Sensor commands to have full control over playback and volume without reaching for your device.

Tips for Effective Use:

- Use deliberate swipes to avoid misinterpreted gestures.

- Ensure your hands are clean and dry for accurate touch detection.

With these touch controls, managing your audio has never been more convenient. The ability to control volume directly from the earbuds eliminates the need for constant interaction with your phone, enhancing your overall listening experience.

Customizing Gestures

One of the standout features of the AirPods Pro 2 is the ability to customize gestures to suit your preferences. Apple provides several options for tailoring the controls to your liking, ensuring the earbuds adapt to your unique usage habits.

Customizing Force Sensor Actions:

1. **Accessing Settings:**

   o Open the Settings app on your iPhone or iPad and navigate to Bluetooth.

   o Tap the "i" icon next to your AirPods Pro 2 to access customization options.

2. **Selecting Actions:**

   o Under the "Press and Hold AirPods" section, choose the desired action for each earbud. Options include:

     ▪ Switching between Noise Control modes (Active Noise Cancellation and Transparency Mode).

     ▪ Activating Siri for voice commands.

3. **Assigning Different Actions to Each Earbud:**

   o Customize the left and right earbuds independently. For example, you can set the

left earbud to toggle Noise Control modes
and the right earbud to activate Siri.

Customizing Touch Controls:

1. **Enable or Disable Features:**

   o While most touch controls are preconfigured,
   you can adjust sensitivity settings through the
   Accessibility menu to ensure they respond to
   your touch as intended.

2. **Integration with Accessibility Options:**

   o For users with specific needs, Apple's
   Accessibility settings allow for adjustments
   such as longer press durations or reduced
   sensitivity.

Using Siri for Hands-Free Control:

1. **Activating Siri:**

   o Say "Hey Siri" to activate the virtual assistant
   without touching the earbuds.

2. **Voice Commands:**

  o Use Siri to control playback, adjust volume, make calls, or check notifications. For example:

    ▪ "Hey Siri, play my workout playlist."

    ▪ "Hey Siri, turn up the volume."

3. **Customizing Siri Responses:**

  o In the Settings app, you can adjust Siri's behavior, such as whether it provides voice feedback or silent responses.

Combining Controls for Maximum Efficiency:

The combination of Force Sensor commands, touch controls, and Siri voice commands creates a highly versatile control system. For example:

- Use the Force Sensor for quick playback adjustments.

- Rely on touch controls for precise volume management.

- Activate Siri for hands-free, complex tasks such as sending messages or setting reminders.

Troubleshooting Control Issues

While the controls on the AirPods Pro 2 are highly reliable, occasional issues may arise. Here's how to troubleshoot common problems:

1. **Force Sensor Not Responding:**

   o Ensure the earbuds are seated securely in your ears.

   o Clean the stems of the AirPods to remove any dirt or debris that may interfere with the sensor.

   o Reset the AirPods Pro 2 by placing them in the charging case, closing the lid for 15 seconds, and then pairing them again.

2. **Touch Controls Not Working:**

   o Verify that touch controls are enabled in the Accessibility menu.

   o Ensure your hands are clean and dry.

   o If the issue persists, restart your connected device or update its software.

3. **Gestures Performing Incorrect Actions:**

   o Check your customization settings in the Bluetooth menu to ensure the gestures are assigned correctly.

   o Reassign gestures if needed and test them in various scenarios.

4. **Siri Not Activating:**

   o Confirm that "Hey Siri" is enabled in your device's Siri & Search settings.

   o Ensure the microphone on your AirPods is unobstructed and functioning properly.

The controls and gestures on the Apple AirPods Pro 2 are designed to provide users with a seamless and intuitive audio experience. By mastering the Force Sensor, touch controls, and customizable gestures, you can tailor the earbuds to suit your preferences and make every interaction effortless. Whether you're adjusting volume with a simple swipe, switching between Noise Control modes, or issuing voice commands to Siri, the AirPods Pro 2 empower you to stay connected and in control without missing a beat. This chapter has provided an extensive guide to understanding and optimizing these controls, ensuring you get the most out of your AirPods Pro 2 experience.

CHAPTER 5

Active Noise Cancellation and Transparency Modes on the Apple AirPods Pro 2

The Apple AirPods Pro 2 stand out in the world of wireless earbuds for their remarkable ability to manage external noise. Whether you want to immerse yourself in your favorite music or remain aware of your surroundings, the Active Noise Cancellation (ANC) and Transparency Modes on the AirPods Pro 2 offer unmatched versatility. This chapter provides an in-depth guide to switching between these modes, optimizing their settings for various environments, and troubleshooting any issues you might encounter.

How to Switch Between Modes

Switching between Active Noise Cancellation and Transparency Mode is quick and intuitive. Apple has designed the AirPods Pro 2 to ensure you can easily toggle between these modes depending on your needs.

Using the Force Sensor:

1. **Toggle Noise Control Modes:**

   o Press and hold the Force Sensor on the stem of either earbud to switch between Active Noise Cancellation and Transparency Mode.

   o A chime will confirm the mode change, helping you know which setting is active without checking your device.

2. **Customize Noise Control Settings:**

   o You can assign specific functions to the Force Sensor through the Settings app on your iPhone or iPad. For example, you can set one earbud to toggle Noise Control modes and the other to activate Siri.

Using the Control Center:

1. **Access the Control Center:**

   o On your iPhone or iPad, swipe down from the top-right corner of the screen to open the Control Center.

2. **Adjust Noise Control Modes:**

   o Press and hold the volume slider. A menu will appear showing options for Noise Cancellation, Transparency, and Off.

   o Select your desired mode by tapping on it.

Using the Settings App:

1. **Open Bluetooth Settings:**

   o Go to Settings > Bluetooth and tap the "i" icon next to your AirPods Pro 2.

2. **Select Noise Control Options:**

   o Under Noise Control, choose between Active Noise Cancellation, Transparency Mode, or Off.

Optimizing Settings for Different Environments

The effectiveness of Active Noise Cancellation and Transparency Mode depends on how you use them in various scenarios. Here's how to make the most of these modes in different environments:

Active Noise Cancellation (ANC):

Active Noise Cancellation is ideal for reducing unwanted background noise, allowing you to focus on your audio without distractions. Here are some tips for optimizing ANC:

1. **Use in Noisy Environments:**

   o ANC works best in environments with consistent background noise, such as on airplanes, trains, or in busy offices. It effectively cancels out low-frequency sounds like engine noise or air conditioning hums.

2. **Ensure a Proper Fit:**

   o For optimal noise cancellation, make sure the earbuds fit snugly in your ears. Use the Ear Tip Fit Test available in the Bluetooth settings to find the best size.

3. **Enable Adaptive Transparency:**

   o Adaptive Transparency automatically reduces the volume of sudden loud noises, such as sirens or construction sounds, while maintaining ANC. This feature can be enabled in the Settings app.

4. **Combine with Spatial Audio:**

   o For a fully immersive experience, enable Spatial Audio along with ANC. This is particularly effective for movies or music where you want to feel completely immersed.

Transparency Mode:

Transparency Mode allows you to stay aware of your surroundings while listening to audio. It's ideal for scenarios where safety or social interaction is important. Here's how to optimize it:

1. **Use in Public Places:**

   o Enable Transparency Mode when walking, cycling, or commuting to stay aware of traffic and other hazards.

2. **Engage in Conversations:**

   o Transparency Mode is perfect for quick conversations without needing to remove your earbuds. It amplifies external sounds, making speech clearer.

3. **Adjust Transparency Settings:**

   o In the Settings app, you can fine-tune Transparency Mode to emphasize specific frequencies, such as voices, for better clarity.

4. **Pair with Adaptive Transparency:**

   o For environments with sudden loud sounds, enable Adaptive Transparency. This feature minimizes the intensity of these noises without compromising situational awareness.

Switching Modes Automatically:

Apple's ecosystem allows for automatic mode switching based on your environment:

- If you're on a call, the AirPods Pro 2 can reduce background noise for clearer communication.

- When pausing audio playback, Transparency Mode can activate automatically, ensuring you're aware of your surroundings.

Common Troubleshooting Tips

Despite their advanced technology, occasional issues with Active Noise Cancellation or Transparency Mode can occur. Here's how to troubleshoot common problems:

1. Noise Cancellation Isn't Working Properly:

- **Check Fit and Seal:** Ensure the earbuds are properly seated in your ears. Use the Ear Tip Fit Test to confirm a secure fit.

- **Clean the Earbuds:** Dirt or debris on the microphone or speaker mesh can affect ANC performance. Gently clean the earbuds with a soft, lint-free cloth.

- **Update Firmware:** Ensure your AirPods Pro 2 are running the latest firmware. Updates are installed automatically when connected to an Apple device with an active internet connection.

- **Restart and Reconnect:** Place the AirPods in the charging case, close the lid, and wait for 15 seconds. Reconnect them to your device and test ANC again.

2. Transparency Mode Sounds Distorted:

- **Adjust Settings:** In the Accessibility menu, fine-tune Transparency Mode settings to improve audio quality.

- **Reset the AirPods:** If the issue persists, reset your AirPods Pro 2 by pressing and holding the setup button on the charging case until the LED flashes amber, then white.

3. Sudden Mode Switching:

- **Disable Automatic Switching:** If the AirPods switch modes unexpectedly, disable automatic switching in the Bluetooth settings.

- **Check Battery Levels:** Low battery can cause inconsistent performance. Ensure both the earbuds and charging case are sufficiently charged.

4. One Earbud Not Cancelling Noise:

- **Inspect the Earbud:** Check for dirt or damage on the affected earbud. Clean it gently to remove any debris.

- **Recalibrate Noise Control:** Remove the earbuds, place them back in the charging case, and reinsert them. This can recalibrate the Noise Control settings.

5. Environmental Noise Still Audible in ANC Mode:

- **Use Adaptive Transparency:** In environments with sudden loud sounds, enabling Adaptive Transparency can enhance ANC's effectiveness.

- **Test in Different Environments:** ANC performs best in consistent noise settings. Test the feature in various locations to confirm its effectiveness.

Tips for Maintaining Optimal Performance

To ensure the long-term effectiveness of Active Noise Cancellation and Transparency Mode, follow these maintenance tips:

- **Regularly Clean Your AirPods:** Keep the speaker mesh and microphones free of dirt and debris.

- **Store Properly:** Use the charging case to protect your AirPods when not in use.

- **Avoid Extreme Temperatures:** High or low temperatures can affect performance. Store your AirPods in a cool, dry place.

- **Check for Software Updates:** Regular firmware updates can enhance ANC and Transparency Mode performance.

The Active Noise Cancellation and Transparency Modes on the Apple AirPods Pro 2 are designed to provide unparalleled control over your audio environment. By understanding how to switch between modes, optimize settings for different scenarios, and troubleshoot common issues, you can fully leverage these features. Whether you're seeking complete immersion or staying connected to your surroundings, the AirPods Pro 2 deliver an audio experience tailored to your needs. This chapter equips you with the knowledge to master these modes, ensuring a seamless and enjoyable experience every time you use your earbuds.

CHAPTER 6

Spatial Audio and Audio Quality on the Apple AirPods Pro 2

The Apple AirPods Pro 2 elevate audio experiences through groundbreaking features like Spatial Audio and the ability to fine-tune sound preferences. These innovations allow users to immerse themselves in dynamic, high-quality soundscapes tailored to their preferences. This chapter provides a detailed exploration of how to set up Spatial Audio, adjust Equalizer (EQ) settings, and optimize your AirPods Pro 2 for the ultimate audio experience.

Setting Up Spatial Audio for Immersive Sound

Spatial Audio is one of the most transformative features of the AirPods Pro 2, delivering a three-dimensional listening experience that makes audio content feel like it's coming from all around you. With dynamic head tracking, Spatial Audio adjusts the sound based on your movements, creating an immersive environment for music, movies, and more.

Step-by-Step Guide to Setting Up Spatial Audio:

1. **Ensure Device Compatibility:**

   o Spatial Audio requires an iPhone, iPad, or Mac with the latest software updates. Ensure your device is compatible and running the most recent version of iOS, iPadOS, or macOS.

2. **Pair Your AirPods Pro 2:**

   o Open the charging case near your device, and follow the on-screen prompts to connect your AirPods Pro 2.

3. **Enable Spatial Audio:**

   o Go to Settings > Bluetooth and tap the "i" icon next to your AirPods Pro 2.

   o Under the Spatial Audio section, toggle the feature to "On."

4. **Personalize Spatial Audio:**

   o Apple allows you to create a custom Spatial Audio profile using your iPhone's TrueDepth camera. Follow these steps:

- Go to Settings > Bluetooth > Spatial Audio Personalization.

- Follow the on-screen instructions to scan your ears and create a profile tailored to your unique auditory preferences.

5. **Test Spatial Audio:**

   o Apple provides a demo to help you experience the difference Spatial Audio makes. Go to Settings > Bluetooth > Spatial Audio and tap "See & Hear How It Works."

Optimizing Spatial Audio for Different Content:

1. **Music:**

   o Use Spatial Audio with supported tracks on Apple Music. Look for the "Dolby Atmos" label to identify compatible content.

2. **Movies and TV Shows:**

   o Stream content from Apple TV+ or other platforms that support Spatial Audio to enjoy a theater-like experience.

3. **Gaming:**

   o Use Spatial Audio with games that support immersive soundscapes for a competitive edge.

Adjusting EQ and Other Audio Preferences

The AirPods Pro 2 provide several options for adjusting audio preferences, allowing users to tailor the sound to their liking. From automatic adjustments through Adaptive EQ to manual control via third-party apps, the AirPods Pro 2 cater to a wide range of preferences.

Adaptive EQ:

1. **What Is Adaptive EQ?**

   o Adaptive EQ uses inward-facing microphones to measure how sound interacts with your ear. It then adjusts the frequencies in real-time for a consistent and high-quality audio experience.

2. **How to Use Adaptive EQ:**

   o This feature is enabled by default and works automatically. You don't need to configure any settings, as the AirPods Pro 2 handle the adjustments seamlessly.

Customizing EQ Settings:

While the AirPods Pro 2 don't have built-in manual EQ settings, you can use the settings on your device or third-party apps to fine-tune audio:

1. **Using iOS Settings:**

    o   Go to Settings > Music > EQ to select a preset that matches your preferences, such as "Bass Booster," "Treble Reducer," or "Loudness."

2. **Using Third-Party Apps:**

    o   Apps like Spotify and other music players often include built-in EQ settings. Navigate to the app's settings and choose an EQ profile or manually adjust frequencies.

3. **Accessibility Adjustments:**

    o   For users with hearing impairments, the Accessibility menu on iOS allows you to fine-tune audio settings:

        ▪   Go to Settings > Accessibility > AirPods.

- Enable "Headphone Accommodations" to amplify soft sounds or adjust frequencies.

Adjusting Volume:

1. **Using Touch Controls:**

   o Swipe up or down on the stem of your AirPods Pro 2 to increase or decrease the volume.

2. **Using Siri:**

   o Activate Siri with "Hey Siri" and say commands like "Turn up the volume" or "Set the volume to 50%."

3. **Using Device Controls:**

   o Adjust the volume directly on your iPhone, iPad, or Mac using the physical or on-screen controls.

Tips for the Best Audio Experience

To get the most out of your AirPods Pro 2, follow these tips to enhance audio quality and optimize your listening experience:

1. Ensure a Proper Fit:

- The fit of your AirPods greatly affects audio quality. Use the Ear Tip Fit Test available in the Settings app to find the best size for your ears.

- A snug fit ensures better bass response and more effective noise cancellation.

2. Maintain Your AirPods:

- Regularly clean the earbuds and speaker mesh with a soft, dry cloth to prevent debris from affecting sound quality.

- Store your AirPods in the charging case when not in use to protect them from damage.

3. Choose High-Quality Audio Sources:

- Stream music in high resolution when available. Apple Music offers lossless audio options for enhanced clarity and depth.

- Use apps and platforms that support Dolby Atmos or Spatial Audio for the best experience.

4. Update Your Firmware:

- Keep your AirPods Pro 2 updated to the latest firmware. Updates often include improvements to sound quality and feature performance.

5. Use Noise Cancellation or Transparency Mode Wisely:

- Activate Active Noise Cancellation in noisy environments to focus on your audio.

- Use Transparency Mode to stay aware of your surroundings without removing the earbuds.

6. Optimize Device Settings:

- Ensure Bluetooth audio codecs are set to high-quality options like AAC for better sound.

- Disable sound enhancements that may conflict with the AirPods' native settings.

7. Explore Spatial Audio Content:

- Apple Music offers curated playlists specifically designed for Spatial Audio. Explore these playlists to experience the full potential of your AirPods Pro 2.

8. Experiment with Audio Settings:

- Don't hesitate to experiment with EQ settings, volume levels, and other adjustments to find what works best for you.

Troubleshooting Audio Issues

Despite the advanced technology, occasional audio issues can arise. Here's how to address them:

1. Audio Sounds Distorted:

- **Clean the AirPods:** Dirt or debris can affect sound clarity. Clean the speaker mesh gently.

- **Check Bluetooth Connection:** Ensure your device is within range and free from interference.

2. Volume Too Low:

- **Adjust Settings:** Increase the volume using touch controls or device settings.

- **Enable Headphone Accommodations:** Amplify softer sounds through Accessibility settings.

3. Spatial Audio Not Working:

- **Check Compatibility:** Ensure you're using content that supports Spatial Audio.

- **Recalibrate Settings:** Go to Bluetooth settings and reset the Spatial Audio profile if necessary.

4. Inconsistent Audio Quality:

- **Reset the AirPods:** Place the AirPods in the charging case, close the lid, and reconnect them to your device.

- **Update Firmware:** Check for firmware updates to resolve potential bugs.

The Apple AirPods Pro 2 set a new standard for audio quality, offering innovative features like Spatial Audio and Adaptive EQ that redefine the listening experience. By setting up these features, fine-tuning audio preferences, and following best practices, you can unlock the full potential of your AirPods Pro 2. Whether you're enjoying music, movies, or calls, this chapter ensures you have the knowledge to achieve the best possible sound quality every time.

CHAPTER 7

Using Siri with AirPods Pro 2

The integration of Siri with the Apple AirPods Pro 2 enhances the user experience by providing hands-free access to Apple's intelligent virtual assistant. Whether you're making calls, controlling music playback, or setting reminders, Siri offers convenience and functionality at your command. This chapter provides a detailed guide on setting up and activating Siri, using hands-free commands, and troubleshooting common Siri-related issues to ensure seamless functionality.

Setting Up and Activating Siri

Before you can use Siri with your AirPods Pro 2, you need to ensure that the virtual assistant is properly set up on your connected device. Follow these steps to get started:

Step 1: Ensure Device Compatibility

1. **Check for Software Updates:**

     o   Ensure your iPhone, iPad, or other Apple device is running the latest version of iOS, iPadOS, or macOS. Go to Settings > General > Software Update to check for updates.

2. **Verify Siri Support:**

   o Siri is available on most Apple devices. Confirm that your device supports Siri by going to Settings > Siri & Search.

Step 2: Enable Siri

1. **Activate Siri Settings:**

   o Navigate to Settings > Siri & Search on your iPhone or iPad.

2. **Enable "Hey Siri":**

   o Toggle on "Listen for 'Hey Siri'" to activate the hands-free wake word feature.

3. **Allow Siri When Locked:**

   o Enable "Allow Siri When Locked" to use Siri even when your device is locked.

Step 3: Connect Your AirPods Pro 2

1. **Pair Your AirPods Pro 2:**

   o Open the charging case near your device, and follow the on-screen prompts to pair your AirPods Pro 2.

2. **Verify Siri Activation:**

   o   Once paired, Siri should be ready to use with your AirPods. Test it by saying "Hey Siri" while wearing your AirPods.

Hands-Free Commands for Calls, Music, and More

One of the standout features of the AirPods Pro 2 is their ability to work seamlessly with Siri for a variety of tasks. Here's a breakdown of common hands-free commands and how to use them:

Making and Managing Calls

1. **Make a Call:**

   o   Say, "Hey Siri, call [contact name]." For example, "Hey Siri, call Mom."

2. **Answer a Call:**

   o   When a call comes in, say, "Hey Siri, answer the call."

3. **End a Call:**

   o   To hang up, say, "Hey Siri, end the call."

4. **Check Voicemail:**

   o Use Siri to access voicemails by saying, "Hey Siri, play my voicemail messages."

Controlling Music Playback

1. **Play a Song or Playlist:**

   o Say, "Hey Siri, play [song name, artist, or playlist]." For example, "Hey Siri, play my workout playlist."

2. **Adjust Volume:**

   o Increase or decrease the volume by saying, "Hey Siri, turn up the volume" or "Hey Siri, turn down the volume."

3. **Skip Tracks:**

   o To skip to the next song, say, "Hey Siri, skip this song."

   o To go back to the previous track, say, "Hey Siri, play the previous song."

4. **Pause and Resume Music:**

   o Say, "Hey Siri, pause" to stop playback, and "Hey Siri, resume" to continue.

Managing Notifications and Messages

1. **Send a Message:**

   o Say, "Hey Siri, send a message to [contact name]: [message content]." For example, "Hey Siri, send a message to Sarah: I'll be there in 10 minutes."

2. **Read Notifications:**

   o Ask Siri to read your notifications by saying, "Hey Siri, read my notifications."

3. **Reply to Messages:**

   o When a message comes in, say, "Hey Siri, reply: [message content]."

Setting Reminders and Alarms

1. **Set a Reminder:**

   o Say, "Hey Siri, remind me to [task] at [time]." For example, "Hey Siri, remind me to pick up groceries at 5 PM."

2. **Set an Alarm:**

   o Use Siri to set alarms by saying, "Hey Siri, set an alarm for [time]."

3. **Check Reminders or Alarms:**

   o Say, "Hey Siri, what are my reminders?" or "Hey Siri, what alarms do I have set?"

Managing Daily Tasks

1. **Get Directions:**

   o Ask Siri for navigation help by saying, "Hey Siri, give me directions to [destination]."

2. **Check the Weather:**

   o Say, "Hey Siri, what's the weather like today?"

3. **Control Smart Home Devices:**

   o Use Siri to manage HomeKit-enabled devices. For example, "Hey Siri, turn on the living room lights."

Tips for Effective Siri Commands:

- Speak clearly and naturally when giving commands.

- Use precise language to ensure Siri understands your request.

- Pause briefly between the wake word ("Hey Siri") and your command for better recognition.

Troubleshooting Siri-Related Issues

If you encounter issues while using Siri with your AirPods Pro 2, follow these troubleshooting tips to resolve common problems:

1. Siri Doesn't Respond:

- **Check Device Settings:** Ensure that "Hey Siri" is enabled in the Siri & Search menu.

- **Ensure Proper Fit:** Verify that the AirPods are seated securely in your ears.

- **Restart Your Device:** Sometimes, restarting your iPhone or iPad can resolve issues.

2. Poor Siri Recognition:

- **Clean the Microphones:** Dirt or debris on the AirPods' microphones can affect voice recognition. Clean the AirPods gently with a soft, lint-free cloth.

- **Reduce Background Noise:** Use Siri in a quieter environment for better recognition.

3. Siri Misinterprets Commands:

- **Refine Your Commands:** Use more specific language to improve Siri's accuracy.

- **Update Your Device:** Ensure your device's software is up to date, as updates often improve Siri's functionality.

4. Siri Stops Working Mid-Session:

- **Check Battery Levels:** Low battery can cause Siri to stop functioning. Ensure both the AirPods and charging case are charged.

- **Reconnect Your AirPods:** Place the AirPods in the charging case, close the lid, and reconnect them to your device.

5. Siri Activation Delays:

- **Reset the AirPods:** Reset the AirPods Pro 2 by pressing and holding the setup button on the charging case until the LED flashes amber, then white. Re-pair them with your device.

6. Siri Not Available in Certain Apps:

- **Check App Permissions:** Go to Settings > Siri & Search and ensure that Siri is enabled for the specific app you're trying to use.

Enhancing Siri's Performance

To get the most out of Siri on your AirPods Pro 2, consider the following tips:

1. **Use Personalized Settings:**

    o   In the Settings app, customize Siri's responses and behavior to suit your preferences.

2. **Leverage Siri Suggestions:**

    o   Enable Siri Suggestions in the Siri & Search menu to receive proactive recommendations based on your usage patterns.

3. **Stay Connected:**

    o   Ensure a stable internet connection, as Siri relies on cloud-based processing for many commands.

Using Siri with the Apple AirPods Pro 2 provides a hands-free, intuitive way to manage tasks, control media, and interact with your devices. By setting up Siri correctly, mastering hands-free commands, and addressing common issues, you can unlock the full potential of this powerful virtual assistant. Whether you're making calls, playing music, or managing your day, Siri ensures you stay productive and connected without lifting a finger.

CHAPTER 8

Battery Life and Charging for the Apple AirPods Pro 2

The Apple AirPods Pro 2 are designed to deliver extended battery life while offering convenient and efficient charging solutions. Understanding how to manage battery levels, utilize fast charging, and maximize battery longevity ensures you get the most out of your AirPods. This chapter provides a comprehensive guide to these aspects, helping you maintain your AirPods Pro 2 in optimal condition.

Understanding Battery Levels and Notifications

Monitoring your AirPods Pro 2's battery life is essential for uninterrupted use. Apple provides multiple ways to check battery levels and receive notifications to ensure you're never caught off guard.

How to Check Battery Levels

1. **On an iPhone or iPad:**

    o   Open the charging case near your device with the AirPods inside.

o A battery status popup will appear on your screen, showing the charge levels of both the AirPods and the charging case.

2. **Using the Batteries Widget:**

   o Add the Batteries widget to your iPhone or iPad's Today View or Home Screen to monitor battery levels in real time.

   o Go to your Home Screen, swipe right, and scroll down to "Edit" to add the widget.

3. **On a Mac:**

   o Click the Bluetooth icon in the menu bar, and hover over your AirPods Pro 2 to view their battery status.

4. **On the Charging Case:**

   o The LED indicator on the case provides a quick battery status:

      ▪ **Green Light:** Fully charged.

      ▪ **Amber Light:** Charging or less than full charge.

Battery Notifications

1. **Low Battery Alerts:**

   o Your AirPods Pro 2 will play a tone when their battery is running low, providing ample time to recharge.

2. **Device Notifications:**

   o Connected devices, such as your iPhone or iPad, will display low battery warnings for both the AirPods and the charging case.

3. **Siri Notifications:**

   o If Siri is enabled, you can ask, "Hey Siri, what's the battery level of my AirPods?" to get an instant update.

Fast Charging Tips

Fast charging is a standout feature of the AirPods Pro 2, allowing you to quickly top up the battery when time is limited. Here's how to make the most of this feature:

How Fast Charging Works

1. **Quick Charge Capabilities:**

   o A five-minute charge provides up to one hour of listening time or talk time.

2. **Optimal Charging Conditions:**

   o Fast charging works best with the Lightning cable connected to a USB-C power adapter rated at 20W or higher.

Charging Methods

1. **Wired Charging:**

   o Use the included Lightning to USB-C cable to connect the case to a power source.

   o For faster results, use a high-wattage USB-C adapter.

2. **Wireless Charging:**

   o Place the MagSafe-compatible charging case on a MagSafe charger or Qi-certified charging pad.

   o Ensure the case's LED indicator lights up to confirm it's charging.

Tips for Effective Fast Charging

1. **Keep Accessories Clean:**

    o   Ensure the Lightning port and wireless charging pads are clean and free from debris for optimal charging performance.

2. **Avoid Overheating:**

    o   Charge in a cool, ventilated area to prevent overheating, which can reduce charging efficiency.

3. **Use Certified Accessories:**

    o   Always use Apple-certified chargers and cables to ensure safety and compatibility.

Maximizing Battery Longevity

The lifespan of your AirPods Pro 2's battery depends on how well you care for and maintain the earbuds and their charging case. Follow these best practices to maximize battery longevity:

General Care Tips

1. **Avoid Extreme Temperatures:**

   o   Exposure to high or low temperatures can degrade the battery. Aim to use and store your AirPods in environments between 32°F and 95°F.

2. **Charge Regularly:**

   o   Avoid letting the battery drain completely before recharging. Regular charging cycles help maintain battery health.

3. **Store Properly:**

   o   When not in use, store your AirPods in their charging case to keep them protected and charged.

Optimize Charging Habits

1. **Enable Optimized Battery Charging:**

   o   This feature learns your charging habits and reduces battery wear by delaying a full charge until you're ready to use the AirPods.

- o Go to Settings > Bluetooth, tap the "i" icon next to your AirPods, and enable "Optimized Battery Charging."

2. **Avoid Overcharging:**

- o While the AirPods case is designed to prevent overcharging, it's good practice to unplug the charger once the battery is full.

Maintain Cleanliness

1. **Clean the Charging Case:**

- o Use a soft, dry cloth to clean the case and remove any dirt or debris from the Lightning port and contact points.

2. **Clean the AirPods:**

- o Wipe the earbuds with a slightly damp cloth and avoid exposing them to liquids or harsh cleaning agents.

Manage Usage Patterns

1. **Use Active Noise Cancellation (ANC) Sparingly:**

- o ANC can drain the battery faster. Turn it off when not needed to conserve power.

2. **Adjust Volume Levels:**

    o Listening at lower volumes can extend battery life during use.

3. **Turn Off When Not in Use:**

    o If you're not using the AirPods for an extended period, disconnect them from your device to preserve battery life.

Troubleshooting Battery Issues

If you encounter problems with your AirPods Pro 2's battery or charging, use these troubleshooting tips:

1. Battery Drains Too Quickly:

- **Check Settings:** Ensure that features like ANC or Transparency Mode are not unnecessarily active.

- **Reset AirPods:** Place the AirPods in the case, press and hold the setup button until the LED flashes amber, and reconnect them to your device.

2. Charging Case Not Charging:

- **Inspect Charging Accessories:** Check the Lightning cable, adapter, or wireless charger for damage.

- **Clean the Case:** Remove debris from the Lightning port using a soft brush or toothpick.

3. Inconsistent Battery Readings:

- **Update Firmware:** Ensure your AirPods Pro 2 are running the latest firmware.

- **Recalibrate Battery:** Fully drain the AirPods and charging case, then recharge them to 100%.

4. AirPods Not Charging in the Case:

- **Check Alignment:** Ensure the earbuds are properly seated in the charging case.

- **Inspect Contact Points:** Clean the metal charging contacts inside the case.

5. Overheating During Charging:

- **Avoid Warm Environments:** Charge the AirPods in a cool, shaded area.

- **Switch Chargers:** Try a different power adapter or wireless charger.

Battery life and charging efficiency are critical aspects of the Apple AirPods Pro 2's performance. By understanding how to monitor battery levels, utilize fast charging, and adopt best practices for battery care, you can extend the lifespan of your AirPods and ensure they're always ready for use. This chapter equips you with the knowledge to manage your AirPods Pro 2 effectively, providing a seamless and reliable audio experience every time.

CHAPTER 9

Maintenance and Care for the Apple AirPods Pro 2

Proper maintenance and care are essential for ensuring the longevity and optimal performance of your Apple AirPods Pro 2. These sleek and technologically advanced earbuds are designed for daily use, but regular cleaning, careful handling, and routine updates are necessary to keep them functioning at their best. This chapter provides an in-depth guide on cleaning and storing your AirPods Pro 2, protecting the case and earbuds from damage, and updating firmware for enhanced performance.

Cleaning and Storing Your AirPods Pro 2

Regular cleaning of your AirPods Pro 2 not only maintains their appearance but also ensures consistent audio quality and hygienic use. Here's how to clean and store your earbuds effectively:

Cleaning the Earbuds

1. **Remove Dirt and Debris:**

   o Use a soft, dry, lint-free cloth to gently wipe the exterior of the earbuds.

   o Avoid using abrasive materials that could scratch the surface.

2. **Clean the Speaker Mesh:**

   o Use a dry, soft-bristled brush to remove debris from the speaker mesh.

   o Hold the AirPods with the mesh facing downward to prevent dirt from falling into the components.

3. **Sanitize the Ear Tips:**

   o Remove the silicone ear tips and rinse them with water. Avoid using soap or harsh chemicals.

   o Let the ear tips air dry completely before reattaching them.

4. **Avoid Liquid Damage:**

   o Do not submerge the AirPods in water or use cleaning agents. While they are sweat- and water-resistant, they are not waterproof.

Cleaning the Charging Case

1. **Wipe the Exterior:**

   o Use a soft, dry, lint-free cloth to clean the outside of the charging case.

   o Avoid getting liquid into the charging port or speaker holes.

2. **Clean the Interior:**

   o Use a soft-bristled brush or a dry cotton swab to remove dust and debris from the inside of the case.

   o Pay special attention to the charging contacts to ensure a good connection.

Storing Your AirPods Pro 2

1. **Use the Charging Case:**

   o Always store your AirPods in the charging case when not in use. This protects them from dust and damage and ensures they stay charged.

2. **Avoid Extreme Temperatures:**

   o Store the AirPods and charging case in a cool, dry place. Avoid exposure to direct sunlight, high humidity, or freezing temperatures.

3. **Transport Safely:**

   o When traveling, use a protective case to prevent scratches and damage to the AirPods and charging case.

Protecting the Case and Earbuds from Damage

Protecting your AirPods Pro 2 and their charging case is crucial for maintaining their appearance and functionality. Here are some practical tips to prevent damage:

Use Protective Accessories

1. **Protective Case Covers:**

   o Invest in a silicone or hard-shell case cover to shield the charging case from scratches and drops.

     o   Choose a cover with a lanyard loop or clip for added convenience and portability.

2. **Ear Tip Replacements:**

     o   Replace the silicone ear tips periodically to maintain comfort and fit. Apple offers replacement ear tips in various sizes.

Avoid Common Hazards

1. **Dropping the AirPods:**

     o   Handle the AirPods and charging case with care. Drops can damage the internal components.

2. **Exposure to Liquids:**

     o   While the AirPods Pro 2 are sweat- and water-resistant, avoid exposing them to excessive moisture or submerging them in water.

3. **Dust and Dirt:**

     o   Keep the charging case closed when not in use to prevent dust and dirt from accumulating inside.

Handle with Care

1. **Open and Close the Case Gently:**

   o   Avoid slamming the case lid or forcing it open. The hinge mechanism is delicate and can wear out with rough handling.

2. **Insert and Remove Earbuds Properly:**

   o   Place the earbuds in the charging case gently to avoid damaging the charging contacts.

3. **Keep Away from Sharp Objects:**

   o   Avoid placing the AirPods or charging case near keys or other sharp objects that could cause scratches.

Updating Firmware for Optimal Performance

Keeping your AirPods Pro 2's firmware up to date ensures you have access to the latest features, bug fixes, and performance improvements. Apple makes the firmware update process seamless and automatic, but there are steps you can take to ensure it happens smoothly.

How Firmware Updates Work

1. **Automatic Updates:**

   o Firmware updates are typically installed automatically when your AirPods Pro 2 are connected to a compatible Apple device with an active internet connection.

2. **Update Prerequisites:**

   o Ensure your AirPods are in the charging case with at least 50% battery.

   o The case should be connected to a power source and paired with your iPhone or iPad.

Checking for Firmware Updates

1. **Access Firmware Information:**

   o Go to Settings > Bluetooth on your iPhone or iPad.

   o Tap the "i" icon next to your AirPods Pro 2 to view the current firmware version.

2. **Verify the Latest Version:**

   o Visit Apple's support website or search online to check the latest firmware version available for the AirPods Pro 2.

Manually Updating Firmware

While firmware updates are automatic, you can encourage an update by following these steps:

1. **Reconnect the AirPods:**

   o Place the AirPods in the charging case, connect the case to power, and keep it near your paired iPhone or iPad.

2. **Wait for the Update:**

   o Leave the AirPods connected for 30 minutes to an hour. The update should install during this time.

Troubleshooting Firmware Updates

1. **Firmware Not Updating:**

   o Ensure your iPhone or iPad is running the latest software.

o Restart both your device and the AirPods to refresh the connection.

2. **Contact Support:**

o If the firmware still doesn't update, contact Apple Support for assistance.

Maintaining and caring for your Apple AirPods Pro 2 is essential for preserving their performance and extending their lifespan. By adopting proper cleaning practices, protecting the case and earbuds from damage, and keeping the firmware updated, you can enjoy a consistently superior audio experience. This chapter equips you with all the tools and knowledge needed to keep your AirPods Pro 2 in pristine condition, ensuring they remain a reliable companion for years to come.

CHAPTER 10

Troubleshooting and FAQs for the Apple AirPods Pro 2

Despite their advanced technology and seamless design, the Apple AirPods Pro 2 may occasionally experience issues that impact performance or functionality. Knowing how to troubleshoot common problems, reset your AirPods, and seek help from Apple Support ensures that you can quickly resolve any issues. This chapter provides an extensive guide to addressing common issues, resetting your AirPods Pro 2, and contacting Apple Support effectively.

Common Issues and Solutions

The following are some of the most frequently encountered issues with the AirPods Pro 2, along with solutions to resolve them:

1. Connection Problems

1. **AirPods Won't Connect to Device:**

    o   **Solution:** Ensure Bluetooth is enabled on your device. Place the AirPods in the charging case, close the lid, and wait 15 seconds. Open the lid and press the setup button on the back of the case until the LED flashes white. Attempt to reconnect.

2. **Frequent Disconnections:**

   o **Solution:** Ensure the AirPods and device are within Bluetooth range. Check for interference from other Bluetooth devices. Reset the AirPods if the issue persists.

2. Audio Quality Issues

1. **Distorted or Muffled Sound:**

   o **Solution:** Clean the speaker mesh using a soft, dry brush. Ensure the ear tips fit properly, and run the Ear Tip Fit Test in the Bluetooth settings.

2. **Uneven Volume Between Earbuds:**

   o **Solution:** Check the balance settings on your device (Settings > Accessibility > Audio/Visual). Reset the AirPods to recalibrate volume levels.

3. Charging Problems

1. **AirPods Not Charging:**

   o **Solution:** Clean the charging contacts in the case and on the AirPods with a soft, dry cloth. Ensure the case is connected to a working power source.

2. **Charging Case Not Charging:**

   o **Solution:** Inspect the Lightning port for debris. Use a different charging cable and adapter to rule out faulty accessories.

4. Noise Cancellation and Transparency Issues

1. **Noise Cancellation Isn't Working:**

   o **Solution:** Ensure Active Noise Cancellation is enabled in the Control Center. Check the fit of the ear tips and clean the microphones.

2. **Transparency Mode Sounds Distorted:**

   o **Solution:** Update the firmware and ensure the AirPods are clean. Reset the AirPods if necessary.

5. Siri Isn't Responding

- **Solution:** Check that "Hey Siri" is enabled on your device (Settings > Siri & Search). Ensure the AirPods' microphones are unobstructed and functioning properly.

Resetting AirPods Pro 2

Resetting your AirPods Pro 2 can resolve many issues, including connectivity problems and inconsistent performance. Follow these steps to reset your AirPods:

How to Reset AirPods Pro 2

1. **Place the AirPods in the Charging Case:**

   - Ensure both earbuds are seated securely in the case.

2. **Close the Lid:**

   - Wait for at least 30 seconds to allow the AirPods to reset internally.

3. **Press and Hold the Setup Button:**

   - Open the lid of the charging case and press the setup button on the back. Hold the button until the LED indicator flashes amber, then white. This indicates that the AirPods have been reset.

4. **Reconnect to Your Device:**

   o Open the charging case near your device. Follow the on-screen instructions to reconnect the AirPods Pro 2.

When to Reset Your AirPods

1. **Frequent Connectivity Issues:**

   o Reset the AirPods if they frequently disconnect or fail to pair with your device.

2. **Audio Imbalances:**

   o Use a reset to address uneven volume levels or distorted sound.

3. **Software Updates Stuck:**

   o If firmware updates fail to install, a reset can help reinitialize the process.

Contacting Apple Support for Help

If troubleshooting and resetting your AirPods Pro 2 do not resolve the issue, contacting Apple Support is the next step. Apple's support team is equipped to assist with complex problems and can provide repair or replacement options if necessary.

Steps to Contact Apple Support

1. **Visit the Apple Support Website:**

   o Go to Apple Support and navigate to the AirPods section.

2. **Describe Your Issue:**

   o Use the search bar or browse through common issues to find solutions. If the issue persists, click "Get Support" to contact Apple directly.

3. **Use the Apple Support App:**

   o Download the Apple Support app on your iPhone or iPad. The app provides step-by-step troubleshooting guides and the option to chat with a support representative.

4. **Call Apple Support:**

   o Dial the Apple Support hotline for your region. Have your AirPods' serial number ready (found on the inside of the charging case lid or in the Bluetooth settings of your connected device).

5. **Visit an Apple Store:**

   o Schedule an appointment at your nearest Apple Store for hands-on assistance. Bring your AirPods, charging case, and proof of purchase.

Warranty and Repair Options

1. **Check Warranty Coverage:**

   o AirPods Pro 2 come with a one-year limited warranty. AppleCare+ extends coverage and includes accidental damage protection.

2. **Repair or Replace:**

   o If your AirPods are under warranty, Apple may repair or replace them free of charge. Out-of-warranty repairs may incur a fee.

Tips for Efficient Support

1. **Prepare Details:**

   o Before contacting support, gather information about your AirPods, including the serial number, firmware version, and a description of the issue.

2. **Be Clear and Concise:**

   o   Clearly explain the problem and steps you've already taken to troubleshoot.

3. **Follow Up:**

   o   Keep a record of your support case number and follow up if the issue is not resolved promptly.

FAQs: Quick Answers to Common Questions

1. **Can I Use My AirPods Pro 2 with Non-Apple Devices?**

   o   Yes, the AirPods Pro 2 can pair with any Bluetooth-enabled device, but some features like Spatial Audio and automatic device switching may not be available.

2. **How Long Does the Battery Last?**

   o   The AirPods Pro 2 offer up to six hours of listening time on a single charge, with an additional 30 hours provided by the charging case.

3. **What Should I Do If My AirPods Are Lost or Stolen?**

   o Use the Find My app to locate your AirPods Pro 2. If they cannot be found, you may be eligible for a replacement through Apple's support program.

4. **Can I Replace a Damaged Earbud?**

   o Yes, individual earbuds can be replaced through Apple's repair service. Fees may apply depending on your warranty status.

5. **How Do I Update My AirPods Firmware?**

   o Firmware updates install automatically when your AirPods are connected to a compatible device with an internet connection.

Troubleshooting and maintaining your Apple AirPods Pro 2 is straightforward with the right knowledge and resources. By understanding common issues and their solutions, knowing how to reset your AirPods, and leveraging Apple Support when needed, you can keep your earbuds functioning flawlessly. This chapter serves as your go-to guide for resolving problems, ensuring a seamless and enjoyable experience with your AirPods Pro 2.

CONCLUSION
Apple AirPods Pro 2 Wireless Earbuds

The Apple AirPods Pro 2 Wireless Earbuds represent a remarkable leap forward in personal audio technology. Designed to combine cutting-edge innovation with ease of use, they offer a versatile and immersive audio experience that seamlessly integrates into everyday life. This user guide has taken you through every aspect of these exceptional earbuds, from unboxing and setup to mastering advanced features and troubleshooting common issues. As we conclude, let's reflect on what makes the AirPods Pro 2 a standout device and how you can continue to enjoy their full potential.

A Revolution in Wireless Audio

Apple's AirPods Pro 2 are more than just earbuds—they are a testament to how far wireless audio technology has come. Featuring the H2 chip, these earbuds deliver superior sound quality, enhanced noise cancellation, and seamless device connectivity. Whether you're a music enthusiast, a professional on the go, or someone who values convenience and innovation, the AirPods Pro 2 are designed to meet your needs.

Seamless Integration with the Apple Ecosystem

One of the defining features of the AirPods Pro 2 is their seamless integration with Apple's ecosystem. From the effortless pairing process to features like automatic device switching and Spatial Audio personalization, these earbuds enhance the user experience across all your Apple devices. With iCloud synchronization, switching between your iPhone, iPad, Mac, or Apple Watch is smooth and intuitive. This level of connectivity ensures that your AirPods Pro 2 are always ready to deliver, no matter which device you're using.

Tailored to Your Lifestyle

The AirPods Pro 2 are designed with versatility in mind, making them suitable for a wide range of activities. Their sweat- and water-resistant design ensures durability during workouts, while features like Transparency Mode and Adaptive Transparency prioritize safety and awareness in public spaces. The customizable controls and gesture options allow you to tailor the earbuds to your preferences, ensuring a personalized experience every time.

Exceptional Sound Quality

At the heart of the AirPods Pro 2 is an audio experience that redefines expectations. The advanced H2 chip powers features like Adaptive EQ, Spatial Audio, and personalized sound profiles, delivering a rich and immersive listening experience. Whether you're enjoying your favorite playlist, watching a movie, or taking a call, the sound quality remains crisp, clear, and balanced.

Mastering Features and Functionality

This guide has explored the numerous features that make the AirPods Pro 2 a standout product:

- **Active Noise Cancellation and Transparency Modes:** These modes ensure that you have control over your listening environment, whether you want to block out distractions or stay connected to your surroundings.

- **Spatial Audio:** With dynamic head tracking and personalized sound profiles, Spatial Audio creates a theater-like experience for music and media.

- **Hands-Free Siri Integration:** Siri provides a convenient way to manage tasks, control playback, and access information without lifting a finger.

- **Battery Life and Charging:** With up to six hours of listening time and fast charging capabilities, the AirPods Pro 2 are designed to keep up with your busy schedule.

Ensuring Longevity

To maintain the performance and longevity of your AirPods Pro 2, regular care and maintenance are essential. By cleaning the earbuds and charging case, protecting them from damage, and keeping the firmware updated, you can ensure that your earbuds remain in optimal condition for years to come. These simple practices will not only preserve their appearance but also enhance their functionality.

Troubleshooting with Confidence

No device is without its occasional challenges, and the AirPods Pro 2 are no exception. However, with the troubleshooting tips and FAQs provided in this guide, you are well-equipped to address common issues and find quick solutions. Whether it's resetting the earbuds, resolving connectivity problems, or seeking support from Apple, you have the resources to keep your AirPods performing at their best.

A Final Word on Innovation

The AirPods Pro 2 embody Apple's commitment to innovation and user-centric design. They combine advanced technology with unparalleled ease of use, making them a benchmark in the wireless earbud market. As you continue to use your AirPods, take advantage of their features and explore their capabilities. Whether you're listening to music, managing calls, or simply enjoying a moment of quiet, the AirPods Pro 2 enhance every aspect of your audio experience.

Moving Forward

As technology continues to evolve, the AirPods Pro 2 remain a testament to how audio devices can transform our daily lives. Their intuitive controls, immersive sound, and seamless integration with the Apple ecosystem make them a valuable companion for work, play, and everything in between. By following the guidance in this user guide, you can unlock their full potential and enjoy a truly exceptional audio journey.

Thank you for choosing the Apple AirPods Pro 2. Whether you're a first-time user or a seasoned Apple enthusiast, we hope this guide has provided you with the knowledge and confidence to make the most of your earbuds. Here's to countless hours of amazing sound and seamless connectivity—a journey that begins with the AirPods Pro 2 and continues wherever your day takes you.

www.ingramcontent.com/pod-product-compliance
Lightning Source LLC
LaVergne TN
LVHW051707050326
832903LV00032B/4056